MILITARY AIRCRAFT

F-22 RAPTOR

BY JOHN HAMILTON

VISIT US AT
WWW.ABDOPUBLISHING.COM

Published by ABDO Publishing Company, PO Box 398166, Minneapolis, MN 55439.
Copyright ©2013 by Abdo Consulting Group, Inc. International copyrights reserved in all
countries. No part of this book may be reproduced in any form without written permission
from the publisher. A&D Xtreme™ is a trademark and logo of ABDO Publishing Company.

Printed in the United States of America, North Mankato, Minnesota.
102012
012013

 PRINTED ON RECYCLED PAPER

Editor: Sue Hamilton
Graphic Design: Sue Hamilton
Cover Design: John Hamilton
Cover Photo: U.S. Air Force
Interior Photos: All photos United States Air Force except: U.S. Navy-pgs 24-25

ABDO Booklinks
Web sites about Military Aircraft are featured on our Book Links pages. These links are
routinely monitored and updated to provide the most current information available. Web
site: www.abdopublishing.com

Cataloging-in-Publication Data

Hamilton, John, 1959-
  F-22 Raptor / John Hamilton.
    p. cm. -- (Xtreme military aircraft set 2)
  Includes index.
  ISBN 978-1-61783-688-6
  1. F-22 (Jet fighter plane)--Juvenile literature. 2. Airplanes, Military--United States-
  -Juvenile literature. I. Title.
  623.74--dc15
                                                        2012945865

TABLE OF CONTENTS

F-22 RAPTOR

★ ★ ★

The F-22 Raptor is flown by the United States Air Force. It is one of the most advanced fighter jets in the world. It uses a deadly combination of stealth, agility, and long range. It can defeat almost any enemy threat.

The F-22 Raptor was built to replace the United States Air Force's F-15 Eagle, one of the most successful fighters of all time.

An F-22 Raptor flies on a training mission over Nevada in 2011.

The F-22 uses high-tech design and electronics. It is unmatched in agility and speed. It is a fearsome dogfighter that pushes the limits of modern technology.

Two F-22 Raptors from Tyndall Air Force Base in Florida fly in formation.

XTREME FACT

The F-22 was designed to defeat such threats as the advanced Russian MiG-29 and Su-35 fighters.

With its stealth ability, most enemies are destroyed before they even know of the F-22 Raptor's presence.

MISSIONS

The F-22 Raptor was built to dominate the skies. Its main mission is air-to-air combat against other planes. With the sky over the battlefield cleared of enemy planes, American ground forces can freely move and attack.

XTREME FACT

The F-22 also has a limited ability to attack enemy ground targets. It uses precision-guided "smart bombs" for such missions.

F-22 Raptors from Langley Air Force Base, Virginia, fly in a training mission.

ORIGINS

In 1981, the United States Air Force began developing a new advanced fighter aircraft. Foreign governments were making fast and deadly modern aircraft.

A YF-22 Advanced Technology Fighter prototype is test flown in 1990. The YF-22 was the forerunner to the F-22 Raptor.

The Air Force needed to match this threat with a new fighter. It would use state-of-the-art materials, engines, weapons, and stealth technology. After a long and costly design and testing period, the F-22 Raptor was the result.

XTREME FACT

Manufactured by Lockheed Martin and Boeing, the first F-22s were deployed by the United States Air Force in 2007. By 2012, a total of 187 F-22 combat fighters were built.

F-22 RAPTOR FAST FACTS

F-22 Raptor Specifications

Function: Fighter aircraft

Service Branch: United States Air Force

Manufacturer: Lockheed Martin, Boeing

Crew:	One
Length:	62 feet, 1 inch (18.9 m)
Height:	16 feet, 8 inches (5.1 m)
Wingspan:	44 feet, 6 inches (13.6 m)
Max. Takeoff Weight:	83,500 pounds (37,875 kg)
Airspeed:	Mach 2+ (1,523 mph/2,451 kph)
Ceiling:	50,000+ feet (15,240 m)
Range:	1,600+ nautical miles (1,841 miles, or 2,963 km)

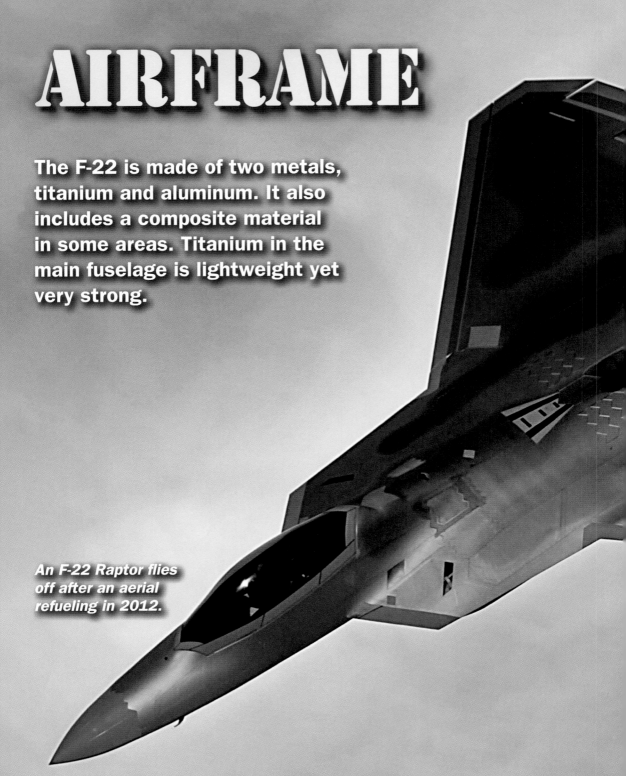

AIRFRAME

The F-22 is made of two metals, titanium and aluminum. It also includes a composite material in some areas. Titanium in the main fuselage is lightweight yet very strong.

An F-22 Raptor flies off after an aerial refueling in 2012.

The F-22's wings are swept back. Their size and shape help make the jet very maneuverable. Fuel is stored inside the wings instead of in external pods. This adds to the aircraft's stealth ability.

STEALTH

The F-22 Raptor's stealth is its greatest strength. It is almost impossible for normal radar to detect the aircraft. Its swept wings and smooth, rounded surfaces minimize radar reflections. Also, a special coating on the aircraft's aluminum and titanium surfaces absorbs radar.

XTREME FACT

The F-22 has a very small radar "signature." On radar screens, the aircraft appears to be the size of a steel marble, making it nearly invisible.

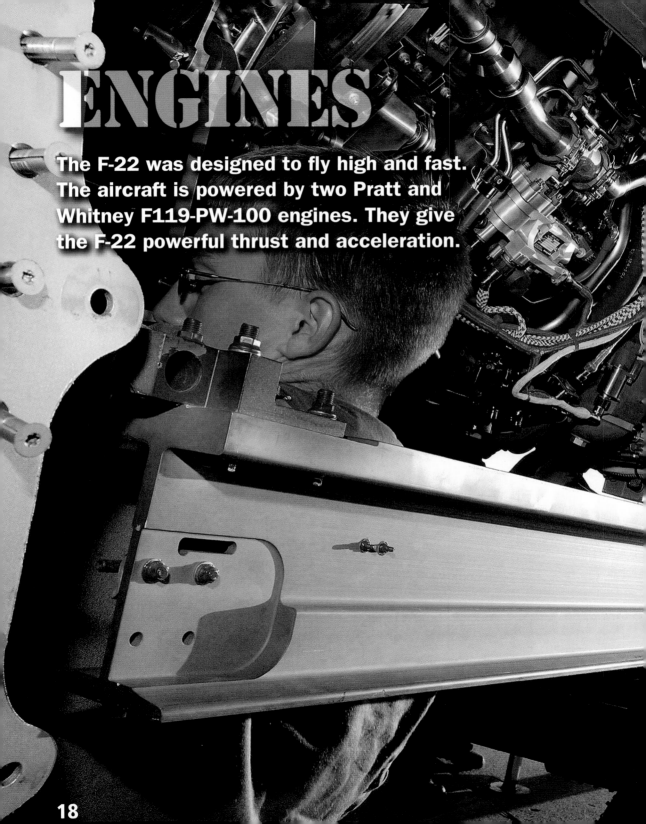

ENGINES

The F-22 was designed to fly high and fast. The aircraft is powered by two Pratt and Whitney F119-PW-100 engines. They give the F-22 powerful thrust and acceleration.

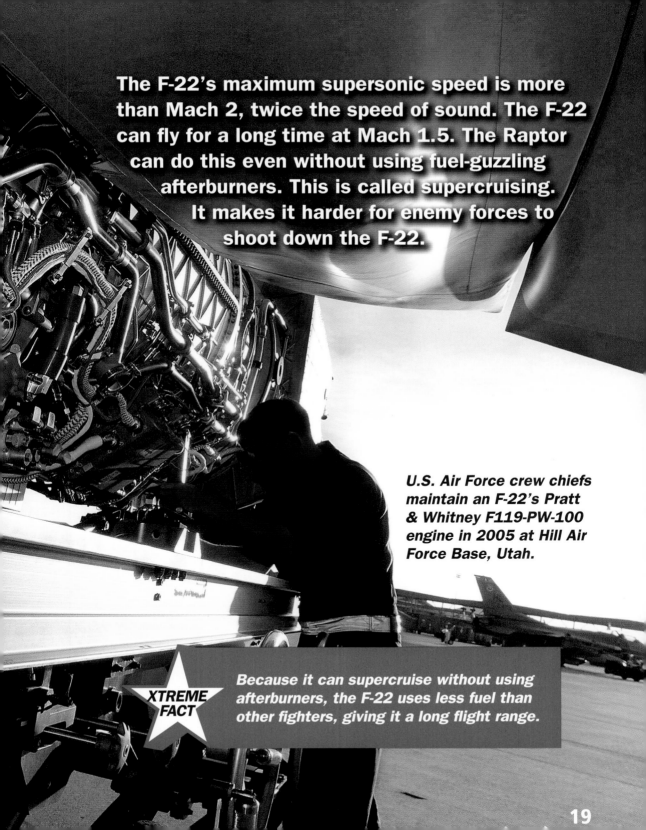

The F-22's maximum supersonic speed is more than Mach 2, twice the speed of sound. The F-22 can fly for a long time at Mach 1.5. The Raptor can do this even without using fuel-guzzling afterburners. This is called supercruising. It makes it harder for enemy forces to shoot down the F-22.

U.S. Air Force crew chiefs maintain an F-22's Pratt & Whitney F119-PW-100 engine in 2005 at Hill Air Force Base, Utah.

XTREME FACT

Because it can supercruise without using afterburners, the F-22 uses less fuel than other fighters, giving it a long flight range.

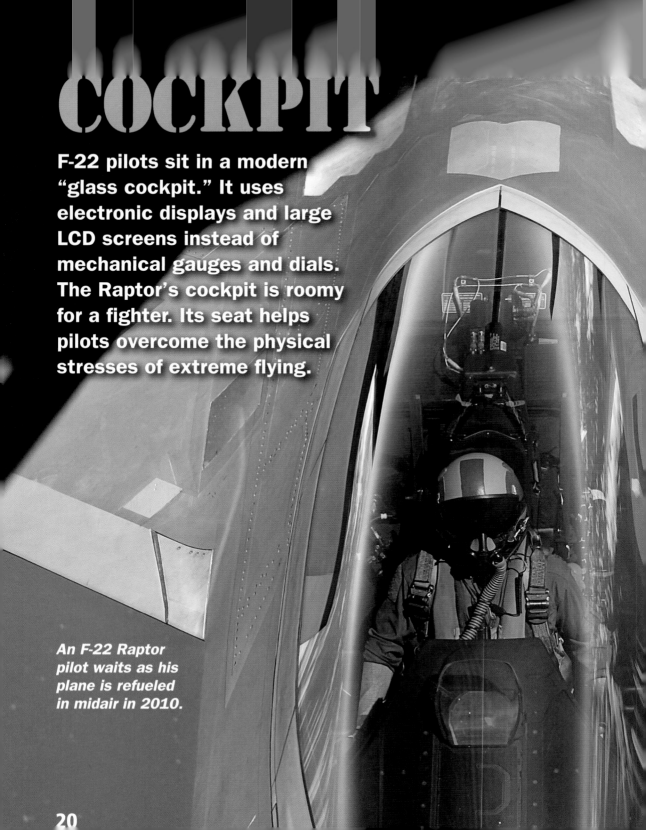

COCKPIT

F-22 pilots sit in a modern "glass cockpit." It uses electronic displays and large LCD screens instead of mechanical gauges and dials. The Raptor's cockpit is roomy for a fighter. Its seat helps pilots overcome the physical stresses of extreme flying.

An F-22 Raptor pilot waits as his plane is refueled in midair in 2010.

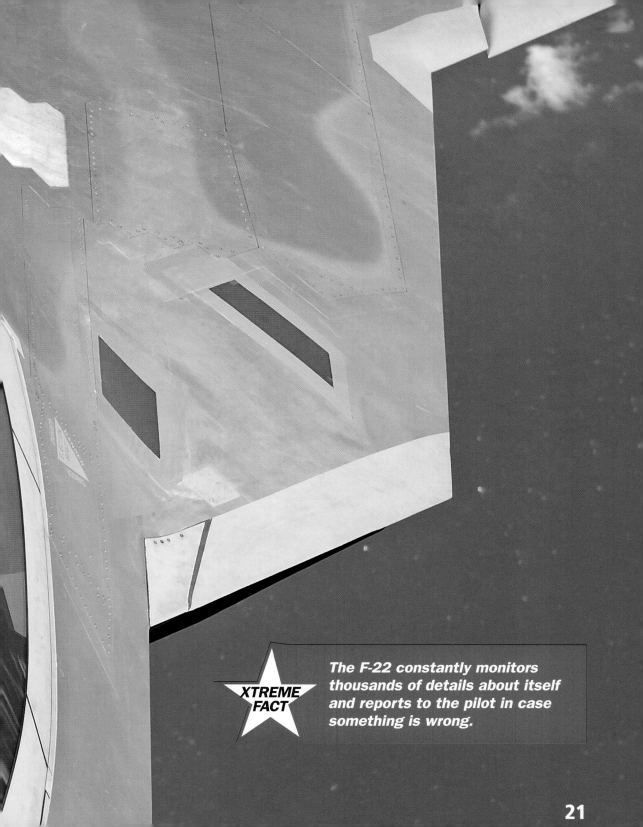

XTREME FACT

The F-22 constantly monitors thousands of details about itself and reports to the pilot in case something is wrong.

AVIONICS

Avionics include all the electronics systems in an aircraft. The F-22 uses some of the most advanced systems available. Radar, communications, weapons sensors, and displays are managed by "integrated" software and hardware. Information is available from a central source. This greatly simplifies the pilot's job.

The F-22's radar can track several enemy targets, even in bad weather. It can also send out focused radar waves to jam enemy radar.

A pilot checks out an F-22 at the Joint Base Elmendorf-Richardson in Alaska in 2012.

WEAPONS

The F-22 Raptor carries missiles and bombs in internal weapons bays. One large compartment is located on the underside of the fighter's fuselage. The other two smaller bays are on the sides of the fuselage.

XTREME FACT

The weapons bay doors are kept closed until needed in flight. This maintains the F-22's stealth ability.

An F-22 with its weapons bay doors open during a demonstration flight in Virginia in 2008.

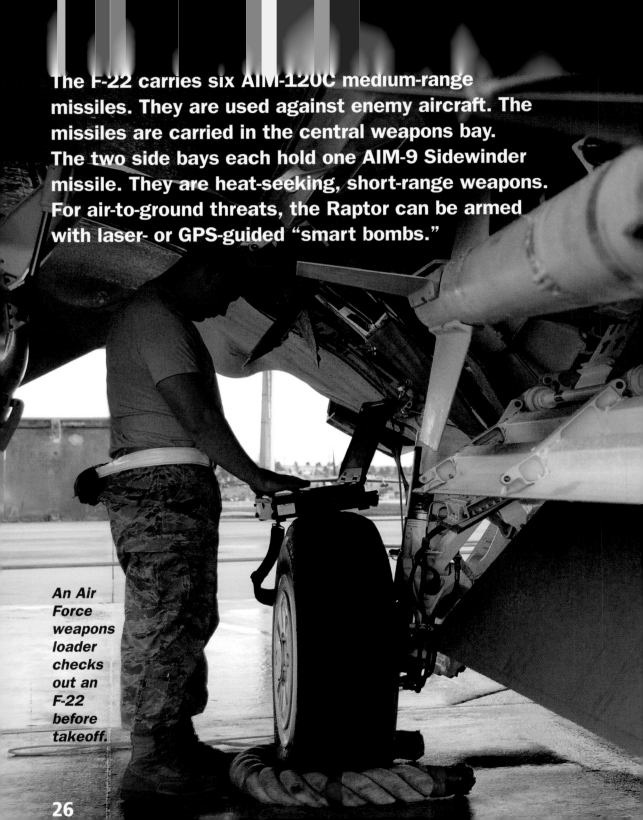

The F-22 carries six AIM-120C medium-range missiles. They are used against enemy aircraft. The missiles are carried in the central weapons bay. The two side bays each hold one AIM-9 Sidewinder missile. They are heat-seeking, short-range weapons. For air-to-ground threats, the Raptor can be armed with laser- or GPS-guided "smart bombs."

An Air Force weapons loader checks out an F-22 before takeoff.

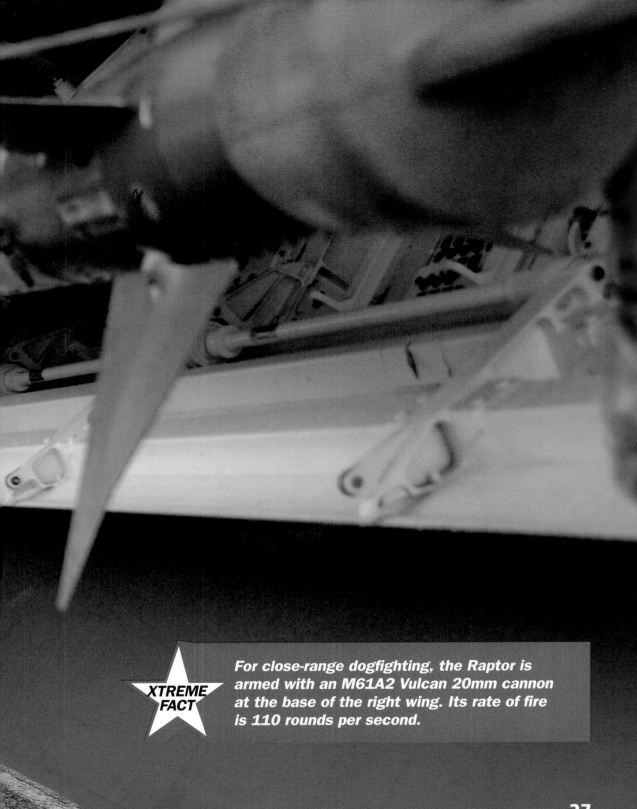

XTREME FACT

For close-range dogfighting, the Raptor is armed with an M61A2 Vulcan 20mm cannon at the base of the right wing. Its rate of fire is 110 rounds per second.

THE FUTURE

The United States stopped making F-22 Raptors in 2009. The F-22 program cost almost $150 million per aircraft. The Air Force decided to build more F-35 Lightning II multirole fighters instead. However, existing F-22 Raptors will serve for many years to come. They will help America control the skies in any future war.

An F-22 Raptor soars over mountains near Joint Base Elmendorf-Richardson, Alaska.

GLOSSARY

AIRFRAME
The body of an aircraft, minus its engine.

AFTERBURNER
A device on a military jet that injects extra fuel into the engine. This provides extra thrust for supersonic flight or in combat. The increased speed comes at the price of consuming much more fuel than normal flight.

COMPOSITE
A strong, lightweight material that blends two or more elements, such as plastic and ceramic resins. Fiberglass and Kevlar are two kinds of composite materials.

FUSELAGE
The main part, or body, of an aircraft that carries the crew and cargo.

A common way to measure the speed of an aircraft when it approaches or exceeds the speed of sound in air. An aircraft traveling at Mach 1 is moving at the speed of sound, about 768 miles per hour (1,236 kph) when the air temperature is 68 degrees Fahrenheit (20 degrees C). An aircraft traveling at Mach 2 would be moving at twice the speed of sound.

MULTIROLE
Able to perform more than one task or mission. The F-22 can attack enemy targets in the air or on land.

NAUTICAL MILE
A standard way to measure distance, especially when traveling in an aircraft or ship. It is based on the circumference of the Earth, the distance around the equator. This large circle is divided into 360 degrees. Each degree is further divided into 60 units called "minutes." A single minute of arc around the Earth is one nautical mile.

RADAR
A way to detect objects, such as aircraft or ships, using electromagnetic (radio) waves. Radar waves are sent out by large dishes, or antennas, and then strike an object. The radar dish then detects the reflected wave, which can tell operators how big an object is, how fast it is moving, its altitude, and its direction.

SUPERSONIC
Moving faster than the speed of sound.

INDEX